DESOLATE COUNTRY

FEATURED TITLES FROM 39 WEST PRESS

Meet the Deplorables: Infiltrating Trump America
by Harmon Leon & Ted Rall

To Act Is To Do
by Richard Alan Nichols

Romoland
by Judith Palmer & Ben Stoltzfus

Where Water Meets the Rock
by Lindsey Martin-Bowen

The Life and Times of José Calderon
by José Faus

Striking the Black Snake: Poems from Standing Rock
MG Salazar

A Secret History of the Nighttime World
Jason Ryberg

Black Girl Shattered
Sheri Purpose Hall

Corazón y una lengua peregrina
Latino Writers Collective

Ghost Sign
Al Ortolani, Melissa Fite Johnson, Adam Jameson, JT Knoll

Nomadic? Rover by Days Singing These Gang Plank Songs of the Ambler
Hugh Merrill

Gender Treason
Ryan Wilks

Tiny Chasm
Jeanette Powers

Undiscovered Paladins: Westward Rhymes Revisited
j.d.tulloch

Fringes
Ricardo Quinones

DESOLATE COUNTRY
we the poets, united, against trump

a 39 WEST PRESS anthology

39 WEST PRESS
Kansas City, MO
www.39WestPress.com

39 WEST
PRESS

Copyright © 2017 by 39 West Press

All rights reserved. No part of this book may be reproduced, scanned, or distributed in any printed or electronic form, including information storage and retrieval systems, without permission. Please do not participate in or encourage piracy of copyrighted materials in violation of the author's rights. Please purchase only authorized editions.

First Edition: January 2017

ISBN: 978-1-946358-02-8

Library of Congress Control Number: 2017900193

This book is a work of fiction. Names, characters, places, dates, and incidents are products of the authors' imaginations, or are used fictitiously, satirically, or as parody. Any resemblance to actual persons, living or dead, business establishments, events, or locales is entirely coincidental.

10 9 8 7 6 5 4 3 2

Design & Layout: Jeanette Powers & j.d.tulloch
Front Cover & Interior Photos: Jenny Wise
Content Editors: MG Salazar, Jen Harris, Jeanette Powers
Edited by j.d.tulloch

39WP-17

"This whole country will become a desolate wasteland, and these nations will serve the king of Babylon seventy years."
Jeremiah 25:11 (NIV)

"The demagogue is usually sly, a detractor of others ... a man who acts in corners ... appeals to passions and prejudices rather than to reason, and is in all respects, a man of intrigue and deception, of sly cunning and management, instead of manifesting the frank, fearless qualities of the democracy he so prodigally professes."

James Fenimore Cooper
The American Democrat (1838)

CONTENTS

Desolate Country
INTRODUCTION   xiii

PART ONE: THE DISENCHANTED

Maryfrances Wagner
ELECTION   3

Gary Lechliter
WHAT JUST HAPPENED?   4

Chico Sierra
LOVE ON ELECTION NIGHT   5

George Wallace
11.9.2016   6

Steph Castor
THE VERDICT   7

Ezhno Martín
HEAVEN IS FALLING   8

Poet Jen Harris
FIRST RESPONSES   10

Miguel M. Morales
DOMESTIC   11

Lonnie Buerge
WOE ARE THEY   12

Mz Angela Roux
WRITE AFTER IT HAPPENED   13

Paul Goldman
THE MORNING AFTER   14

Philip Hooser
HOUSE   15

Mark Matzeder
GUERNICA   16

Crista Siglin
HOROSCOPES   18

James P. McNamara
I HAD KNOWN   20

Mz Angela Roux
SOUR NOTE   21

.chisaraokwu. (naijabella)
MORNING IN SALERNO   22

Jim McGowin
UNDER AN EMPYREAN SKY   23

PART TWO: THE DISDAINFUL

George O. Martin
MASSIVE STRENGTH   27

Ezhno Martín
BATHESHEBA   28

Kathleen Gullion
MAKE AMERICA QUEER AGAIN   30

Kevin James
THE DONALD — 31

Mark Manning
TRUMP RANTS — 32

Abe Fernandez
DEAR DONALD TRUMP — 34

Kevin James
TRUMP & HIS BLOODSUCKERS — 36

Kevin James
T-RALLY — 37

Kyle Laws
IN ATLANTIC CITY — 38

Jill Karno
THESE BURIED HEARTS — 39

Nadia Wolnisty
HOW THE LIGHT GETS IN — 40

Ezhno Martín
HELL IS IN THE HEARTLAND — 42

Maryfrances Wagner
NOVEMBER AFTERMATH — 44

Alisha Escobedo
ANOTHER MODERN DECLARATION — 45

Emma Fernout
LETTERS — 46

Jason Preu
RE: HATING YOU — 48

PART THREE: THE DISENFRANCHISED

.chisaraokwu. (naijabella)
MY BLOOD FLOWS RED — 55

MG Salazar
MY ANCESTORS' BLOOD — 56

Miguel M. Morales
THIS POEM ISN'T — 57

Jessica Ayala
SEEDS — 58

Iriquois Pliskin
A LETTER TO PRESIDENT OBAMA — 60

Keith D. Wilson
RISING UP — 62

Iris Appelquist
DON'T BE A FUCKING RACIST — 64

Alisha Escobedo
THE POWER OF PUSSY — 65

Nichole Force
BOXING HILLARY — 66

Andrea Caspari
A STUDENT DREW A SWASTIKA ... — 68

Kathryne Husk
AKTION T4 — 70

James Inman
REPUBLICANS V. DEMOCRATS — 73

Paul Oldham
MUCH WORSE 74

Benjamin Rosenthal
THIS IS ... 76

Ezhno Martín
IN JUNK YARD DOGS WE TRUST 77

CC Grooms
THE EMPEROR'S NEW CLOTHES 78

Max Martin
SAINT JUDE THADDEUS 79

Desolate Country
INTRODUCTION

For many of us, the outcome of the November 2016 presidential election has spawned visceral and painful reactions, including passionate social media pleas and protests in the streets. Our friends and loved ones have expressed thoughts of fear, anxiety, and hopelessness; families have crumbled under the pressures of disagreements.

We are a polarized nation in need of uniting. In an attempt to provide hope during this time of discontent, 39 West Press presents *Desolate Country: We the Poets, United, Against Trump*, a social justice anthology designed to embrace multiculturalism and diversity by empowering those who have been disparaged by the President-elect's vile rhetoric of xenophobia, Islamophobia, homophobia, bigotry, misogyny, and hate.

Now, more than ever, our collective voices (and actions) must stand united in opposition to Donald J. Trump, who—by following the demagogue's playbook—seeks to divide and conquer by turning Christians against Muslims, white folks against people of color, men against women, and straights against LGBTQIAs, thereby creating fear and hate amongst the populace.

While these calculated tactics seek to destroy the fundamental institutions of democracy and lead *We the People* to quarrel and vilify each other, Trump—without opposition—slyly invokes his true agenda: the marginalization of the masses and the continued facilitation of the advancement and concentration of wealth of the most affluent members of our society, which is evidenced by his billionaire cabinet nominees and bizarre infatuation with Russian President (and evil) Vladimir Putin, who had a direct role in hacking the presidential election by authorizing malicious cyber-attacks designed to boost Trump and damage Hillary Clinton.

This collection, therefore, represents an amalgamation of defiant work by established artists and others who, as a result of Trump's *election*, were inspired to write in protest. It aims to give voice to believers in the power of art to act as both a spiritual catharsis and an agent of change while also empowering each person who is morally opposed to saying, "Trump is my President."

PART ONE
THE DISENCHANTED

Maryfrances Wagner
ELECTION

A blackened oval and the room
shifts. Memory like lost wax
forgets its old brass master.

Once you were the blind date fill in,
the guest invited because of someone else.

Everything sidesteps your line of vision
in that blind spot from your side mirror.

You're the one left standing
when all the chairs fill, the lone
raised hand in a sea of faces.

Behind your back, empires
have been erected. Silence

pounds through your ears
in bruising shell rush, rumbles
through you in queasy void.

Gary Lechliter
WHAT JUST HAPPENED?

Understanding does not cure evil, but it is a definite help, inasmuch as one can cope with a comprehensible darkness. –Carl Jung

Needing something to break the tension as the polls closed, we went to a movie and now cannot remember the title, who played whom, nor the plot and ending. Afterward, we ate at our favorite café. It all seemed normal, as it should be. Surely, we said, our country will progress.

But when we returned home to watch the votes roll in, hopeful for the futures of our grandchildren and their children, we sat there stunned, as if the world were ending, as if fate had sucker-punched us. At that moment, the earth was off kilter and gravity slipped a stitch.

The laws of physics were rendered null. Maybe the earth is truly a pancake, not some chubby little orb on which we spin. Sense and responsibility packed their bags and took the first flight to anywhere that values the worth of the soul and loves the rare, sleek skin of difference.

The night and the solar shadow's idea of the moon had rotted all its cheese. There was a rustle among the ghosts. The neighborhood gnomes wept and pissed in their shoes. Something moved hard through the trees: the dry limbs of cottonwood bending, breaking.

We knew that elections are rough-hewn; so, in the finest scotch we sobbed for what will occur during the next four years, which cannot be corrected with regrets. Our old bed cried to be slept on. And try to sleep we did, thrashing like helpless carp thrown on the bank to rot.

Chico Sierra
LOVE ON ELECTION NIGHT

We were warm
With optimism

Holding hope
Between us

Like a sleeping child
We watched

As the worst
Of us had their way

The moon hung
So low

That we felt
The tide turn

As we tried to sleep

George Wallace
11.9.2016

All things are quite silent (a dreadful silence everywhere)
America is a hospital waiting room

It is 2:30 a.m.
a wall clock's ticking.

Steph Castor
THE VERDICT

You killed a bottle of vodka.
I sipped shit Pinot from a box ...

... but not before wisecracking and smashing a few cans:
sweating cylinders of "America."

Neither of us knew how to focus
on each other.

Yet when the temperature bowed out,
we never loved harder,

huddling together,
rocking, on the concrete.

Kansas City always looks dead
in the dark—

the silence
in the bar across the street

the lack of echoes
in the presumed gunfire

the skyscrapers slowly dimming
their patriotic flickers to a sunken orange.

Ezhno Martín
HEAVEN IS FALLING

        The pagans are betraying their savage nurture
wild wailing and gnashing their teeth at the news
            The Lord has chosen his new leader
       and it isn't their Whore of Babylon
            but a second coming of King David
       sent to restore the throne to the chosen
and wage war by God's grace
                to purge the land of trespassers

       I welcome the brimstone rains
           because it's only heaven falling
    I've been following my lucky seven stars
            and soon all seven seals will be open
         We'll all be dead before you know it
                and my faith keeps me unafraid

       Our new Caesar prophesies that all the holy
will receive their riches soon
            and never suffer a second death
     so long as they die the first for their fidelity
           the valley in the shadow of death can be filled
to the sun with bodies
              but our souls are eternal in paradise
and our names will remain in the book of life
        even as all the others are blotted out
               God is shaking the half
changed sinners
            and Satan's spies from the clouds
                  they explode when
they hit the ground
            all that noise is just heaven falling

When we overcome
the doomed will know us
            as the ones pure and white
    when the condemned beg for mercy
            we'll remind them they're damned
    because envy made them fight
we would have let them live
            had they accepted slavery on their knees
    but they wanted equality
                    so only in hell will they be bereaved

    Heaven is falling
            thank God heaven is falling
all that anguished caterwauling
            is only the cost of greed
    when heaven is falling.

Poet Jen Harris
FIRST RESPONSES: THE PROGRESSION OF A MELTDOWN OR THE DAY I HATED AMERICA

November 8 · 11:29pm · Overland Park, KS
I am so fucking disgusted with this country right now. If I wasn't trapped in this hospital you'd better believe I'd be ready to riot.

November 8 · 11:49pm · Overland Park, KS
Just so we're clear: Hitler and Trump are both Nationalists.

November 9 · 3:34am · Overland Park, KS
Just so we're clear: this means war, and it will not be on us this time.

November 10 · 6:08am · Overland Park, KS
Anyone who accepts Trump in real life or shows even the slightest pacifism via Facebook status is henceforth an enemy of mine. We've already seen you throughout history. You let the Holocaust happen. You let Anne Frank die in an attic. You have armed mass murders and forced women into the role of property. You revealed the elaborate tunnels of the Underground Railroad. You traded in your god for 30 pieces of silver. We will trample over you at the front lines.

*Edit for people who don't read between my lines. Anne Frank lost her life in a camp; she died in an attic. The loss of freedom is death. Additionally, the Underground Railroad was not actually a series of tunnels. These are called metaphors. I am Poet. It's what I do.

Miguel M. Morales
DOMESTIC

Anyone who voted for Donald Trump
is no better than the monster who walked
into Pulse Nightclub on Latin Night and
single-handedly killed 49 queer people.

You are no better than the domestic terrorists
who car-bombed the federal building in
Oklahoma City. You killed 168 people
including 19 children — babies.

You killed 20 more children and six teachers
at Sandy Hook Elementary School.
You roamed the halls full of rage shooting
first graders huddled in bathrooms and in closets.

You sat in Mother Emanuel in Charleston,
studied scripture and prayed with the Black worshipers.
After shooting them, in hopes of starting a race war,
you grabbed a burger with your arresting officers.

With a concealed carry handgun license serving
as your voter ID, you stepped into the voting booth,
carefully targeted the most vulnerable, and with
satisfaction you pulled the lever imagining it as a trigger.

On Election Day, these traitors, these conspirators,
these deplorables coordinated their Christian right,
radical white supremacist agenda and initiated a
terrorist attack on the   United   States of America.

They belong   in jail.
                              Lock them up.

Lonnie Buerge
WOE ARE THEY

Woe are they who have
sold the souls
of the faithful
for a thrilling touch
of the silk garments
of power;
they have pimped
their jesus
for a few pieces
of silver and gold;
they have traded
their vision
for blinders
and taken
on the cloaks
of evil
for the chance
to stand
in the ante rooms
of privilege
for their own gains.
And, forsaking God
and the commandments
to serve the poor
to wash the feet
of the traveler
and to feed
the hungry,
their voices
are now like
clanging cymbals
and hollow
trumpets filled
with bile and waste.

Mz Angela Roux
WRITE AFTER IT HAPPENED

America was assassinated last night
In front of a live studio audience
No laugh track
No red light to prompt for applause

Pause!

Welcome to An American Horror Story
A Star Spangled Freak Show
Step right up!
To the greatest lie on Earth
Starring a cast of Bearded Bitches! Bedazzled Jackasses!
And Ego-maniacal Elephants!
In a cosmic duel to conjure the illusions of
Life, liberty and the pursuit of Nielsen ratings
A riot is going on outside
A coven of conservatives behead the doves
While you binge-watch your favorite TV show

America was assassinated last night
In front of a live studio audience
No one laughed
No one applauded

Paul Goldman
THE MORNING AFTER

I sit here amongst the crumpled sheets, filled with the tears
of millions upon millions of my sisters and brothers, asking
where is love, asking what has happened to good conscience,

grace, and a deep abiding compassion for all peoples, which
was once our guiding principle? Like adolescents waking up
with changing bodies and raging hormones, here in this

questionable morning after, our tentative voices rise up
above the fray, chanting, "Who am I now?" Where do we go to
begin? Slogging through the fog at first, knowing that even in

this murky scene, love is still here; she has not fled—nor can
she ever. It is you and I—we are the ones—who will be the
progenitors of an even deeper love (of peace's potential) and

perhaps even the harbingers of a new understanding. As
the sun still rises, love—sweet persistent love—still courses
through us, embracing our unity and sending every scintilla

of separation to the ash heap. Though we may cry and our
hearts may be heavy with grief, this morning after we
must turn to face each other, in love with love again.

Philip Hooser
HOUSE

I am sitting in a house.
I have always lived here.
My neighbors have set my house on fire.
I am sitting, waiting.
The fire may grow and engulf me.
And it may swallow them, too.
But I do not know.
I watch the flames glow and grow
While each new ember of the team
Seems worse than the one before.
I will wait to see what happens.
No one knows.
It may be nothing.
It may blow over.
Besides, my chair
By the window is comfortable.
From here,
I watch my neighbors dance and chant
How they have won.
It is fire.
I am only one person.
Fire has a long history and a will of its own.
I just have to accept that.

Mark Matzeder
GUERNICA

There will be no poem today ...

My Muse is deep in mourning
Garments rent, face bathed in ashes
For Fraternité brought home
Broken on his shield.
She's banned from giving proper pyre
Or placing Charon's coin upon his eyes
To lay him in the ground.
Condemned to watch our Beloved
Rot in public, wrought in shame,
Wrought by actions of our kin,
Intended or no he's just as dead.

There will be no poem today ...

My Muse's heart is sot with pain
For babies bruised and broken
And wives bereft of young
In the wake of thundering hoofsteps
Death and Famine, War, Disease
Unloosed at the Trumpet's calling
Opened up their floodgates wide
Gushing tide of filthy hate
Oozing like a bubo pustule
Bursting from the People's flesh.

There will be no poem today ...

My Muse is gone, who knows how long
The Reichstag registered and branded her: *Verboten!*
They deemed her degenerate
And you were not degenerate,
You did Nothing

So she's been carted off to earn
Her Freedom through Work
Writing copy for cheap trinkets
You'll swallow by the handfuls
While Don Draper and Gordon Gekko
Fellate each other on the floor.

There will be no poem today ...

Or tomorrow or tomorrow or tomorrow
My Muse cannot thrive this Mad Max world
Burning corpse of hope
Smoldered ruin of dream
Scorched earth celebration of barbarity
Human inhumanity.

We shout to the Abyss,
"What have you done?"

And hear Its whispered echo,
"No. You did."

Crista Siglin
HOROSCOPES

we hear each other's heads' insides
clenching our teeth privately while aloud

we're referencing obscure horoscopes—those texts
written on the roofs of our mouths—

maybe it is melancholia—or perhaps excuses
to remove ourselves from our daddies

all gods
made up yet so real

we each used to ask particular daddy gods
daddies, "can we eat dinner now?"

daddies, "am I pretty now?"
daddies, "am I a man now?"

after we grew some
we grew bolder

asked the daddies,
"must all our heroes be dead?"

although, we really meant
must they all die so violently?

without answer
we become scrapes and bruises spread on our parts

we may know beauty
but it cannot distinguish us from the world

we feel foreign (and indifferent)
as we are everything we've known

we are violent too
(imagine killing daddies)

but when it feels impossible
we blame the wilderness of nameable stars

James P. McNamara
I HAD KNOWN

I had known this to walk into the room and consume no space: ever present as the saints are said to be.

      And yet ...

I had known this viciousness. That choices here cut in kind too. That this consensus was spirit photography.

      And yet ...

I had known this to be the mitral valve mitigating the pace at the center of this flush cheeked beast.

      And yet ...

I had known this extraction. The bloody root has busted a snout loose of the shale toothed soil.

It never slept but soaked the pulse of its life, a thread from our darker paranoia confirmed.

Predictably adrift in the shivering fault lines, adding iron to the marrow and padding to the paw.

I had known. I had known. I had known these so deeply.

That hubris and malaise did dance so commonly, so diametrically that they could collide and shift closer to that final shore.

I had known this to be us four years ago and four years before.

      And yet ...

Mz Angela Roux
SOUR NOTE

we tried to synth it away
found ourselves
swinging aimlessly from
cranes in the sky
ready to fall free
into the crates of soul records
that scratch beyond the surface
of our pain.

.chisaraokwu. (naijabella)
MORNING IN SALERNO

The morning after the ballots were cast, spirits found their way to a darkened hole

A people woke up to a morning bathed in haloed light just as they had for millennia

The sun wrapped itself in a rainbow-colored cloud, dressed itself in a deep sky blue, and warmed the souls of old men

Children with brightly colored backpacks and black sneakers eagerly ran ahead of their parents just for the chance to look back and see them still sanding there

The stop lights changed from red to green every forty-five seconds while the waves continuously crashed upon the sand

The morning after the ballots were cast, the sun refused to change its course and shined upon us all the same

The world continued to spin

And some of us will choose to see this differently.

Jim McGowin
UNDER AN EMPYREAN SKY

Reality can be a cold place,
    Feigning both beauty and benevolence
To sucker in all of us lovers and dreamers.
    Under an empyrean sky we dozed,
Until a cruel awakening, an unimaginable joke,
    Catastrophic and hellish in its bent,
Left us staring into our untouched coffees.
    Kamikaze broadcast apostles
Proved exactly how crazy people can be, proved
    Truly that ignorance is a blissful Judas kiss
For brutish denizens drunk on Internet snake oil,
    Reveling in the absurdity
Of their contrarian paper-tiger convictions.
    Under an empyrean sky we dozed,
Tried to dream up some sort of rationality,
    Making dressings for all the bleeding wounds,
Only left assured of one thing:
    Pulling ourselves up out of the dirt
Must never become merely an option.

PART TWO
THE DISDAINFUL

George O. Martin
MASSIVE STRENGTH

There is something about the beast
We secretly love. We really want to be
The bear mother, step out of the kitchen
Where there is no food, and ravage the camp
Next door. There are times we want to be
The devil himself and laugh as we strike down
The loyal opposition and blind affiliates.
Didn't you want to be the miss-understood
Frankenstein monster and be left alone?
Weren't you in accord with the ignorant
Student that the teacher berated?
Sometimes we want to be the monster
Because, secretly, we want to win.

Wouldn't you just once like to breathe fire,
Like the dragons of myth? Or the shark
With teeth and jaw that can rip the one
Who just ripped you, for nothing other
Than being you? I have wanted to be
The Ogre living under the bridge; I could
Leap out unexpectedly and take my toll
As the aggrieved, as the wronged, as the hurt.
I have wanted to be the animal with acid
Tongue and vitriol behind it to scar the face,
The flesh of my nemesis. I have wanted the
Strength of a lion, the cunning of a wolverine,
But I am a sheep of the fold. He feeds me.

Ezhno Martín
BATHESHEBA

        You saw me bathing
and I
      not even naked
could feel your heat on my skin
            before I knew you were watching

Sending for me was only a formality
            there would be guards and spears
if the messenger wasn't pleased
      so I told him he could watch
me finish getting clean for you
           but only if it satisfied him
      I only wanted to wash the blood out of myself
           so as to lay a trap in the hole
I knew you would be using like it was a handle
           to jerk me and my family around with

      You were the King suddenly
and I was resigned to you killing my husband
      just as soon as the details were signed
so I decided
           then and there
      that if you were going to rape me
              with the glad-handing caress
      of property that can be manhandled without
           permission
      I'd keep you for a few rounds
      so I'd have enough seed inside me
           that you'd have a son
      who one day would come to take your throne
           like you had decided to take me
      like a sacrifice
to sins you'd never be blamed for

                I raised my ass to you
not only because it was the easiest way to pretend I liked it
              but also because I couldn't stand to face you
                                knowing I'd see you
                        in our son's face forever
                                    and all women can do
              is build a better future out of our tragedies

                There was no changing that Goliath fell
(maybe by sabotage)
                    so you were charged with our destiny
                    and not because you were powerful
(your wig of Sampson's fallen hair fooled no one)
              but because you were scared and full of poison

                        Even I told you
                            when you asked me if it felt good
                                    knowing surrendering to
meant prospering with the King
                        that I knew you
              as just the kind of boisterous little boy
              with delicate small hands
              who'd accepted deep down that he'd never be big

You put your seed in me anyway
          and I asked you for more
because on your borrowed time
          it was the battle I knew I'd always win
precisely by proving
                        that you were empty
God's vessel
                and I was full with fecundity
            and future I could control
                        more than even you.

Kathleen Gullion
MAKE AMERICA QUEER AGAIN

I think Donald Trump is a top ... and not in the way where he gets satisfaction from giving other people pleasure ... and not in the way where he consensually seduces you into submission. He's a top in the way where its the only way he knows how to be. He may have read the Kama Sutra in college, but missionary is still his favorite position. He takes off his socks off and leaves on his shirt. He turns off the lights before mounting you like a neutered dog. He won't look deeply into your eyes. He won't softly say your name into your ear, tickling the peach fuzz on your earlobe. Instead, he'll scream out, "Bitch motherfucker shit goddamn fuck," after without lube he penetrates you for approximately 45 seconds. He'll shudder and cum inside you, condomless, peel himself out of you, and then light a cigarette. He won't offer you one.

I wish Donald Trump were a bottom. I want him to blush with anticipation as you slowly unbutton his starchy, white button-down shirt, one button at a time. I want him to give up control and let you take the reins. I want him to enjoy getting slammed against a bookcase every now and again, especially on Wednesday afternoons. I want him to know what he likes and have the courage to ask for it. And just because he's submissive, it doesn't mean that he has to be passive. I want him to think "pillow princess" is a compliment, not a pejorative. I want him to say, "Yes," because he means it, and I want him to scream your name at the height of passion because of the exquisite feelings you give him. I want him to start doing yoga so that he can learn how to put his legs behind his head. I think he'd like that, and I think you would too. Afterwards, you both will share cigarettes, Marlboro Southern Cuts, and if you don't smoke, then you'll eat salsa and tortilla chips instead. They won't be too salty, no. They'll be perfect.

Kevin James
THE DONALD

He's the kind of guy, like Henry VIII,
   from whom you try to hide your women,
to whom you might bow as he goes by
   but would spit at or pick a fight with
if he weren't richer, who swoops away
   in his black Armani and Rolls, who bites
each coin and riffles each fat-banded cash stack
   like Uncle Scrooge McDuck, swimming
in lucre, in gold wave troughs and crests.
   Some guys are fucked by all the luck.

Mark Manning
TRUMP RANTS

#1: I WILL NOT ACCEPT DUMP TRUCK AS MY PRESIDENT
I will not accept Dump Truck as my President. NEVER!!! I will not forgive those who voted to support his racism, sexism, and hate. I will not forgive those who did not vote or voted for a third party candidate with absolutely no chance of winning, You helped elect a horrible man. I will not forgive the evangelical voters who proved to me that their religion is based on extreme hypocrisy. I am in shock and misery, and I am embarrassed to call myself American. Good bye equality. Good bye Supreme Court. Good bye healthcare. Good bye environment. Good bye to our nation's respect from the rest of the world. Good bye to our nation's self respect. Waking up, after last night's sad tragedy, to such a clearly divided nation, so obviously divided on racial lines, leaves me shaking in disbelief. The American Dream has now been replaced with the American Nightmare as the obstructionist party of "no" now takes total control over all three branches of our government. This is so very sad. The next four years will be a constant stream of protest from me. For those who cast their vote for a sexual predator, don't ever expect me to sit at your table.

#2: I HAD NIGHTMARES ABOUT ROSIE O'DONNELL
Last night, I had nightmares about Rosie O'Donnell being tortured in the public square, and then, I woke up and realized that a sick, racist sexual predator is now our President, elected by an almost 100 percent white and evangelical vote. And my nightmare continues. Now, I will unplug the TV that created and shoved this Trump monster down our throats, and I will sit back and watch a political party in control of everything, with no one to blame but their own ugly selves. I will continue to devote my energy to all the work I'm already doing. I don't have time for American Political Theatre; I'm just not that good of an actor. My faith and work have always been with children,

artists, musicians, community airwaves, and our environment. That won't change. But when it comes to a Trump Presidency, I will not forget those who have allowed this to happen.

#3: TODAY AT THE ELEMENTARY SCHOOL
Today, at the elementary school where I did workshops, teachers told me about how difficult this week has been not only for their own states of mind but especially for the immigrant children they serve. I heard stories about how entire classrooms of little kids have been crying openly out of fear that someone might come into their homes and take their fathers away. This is what the election of Donald Trump means for our children. This is what the ignorant voters who have elected a racist, sexual predator have created through their hate. It just breaks my heart. America has broken my heart.

Abe Fernandez
DEAR DONALD TRUMP

Mr. Trump,

Do you know the injustice you impose on not only Mexicanos but on *La Raza*?

Have you ever met a Mexican worker, ever? We are not a people of rapists nor drug addicts. The Mexican people, Latinos and Latinas, *La Raza* are some of the hardest working people in this god damn country. But you wouldn't know anything about hard work.

You were born with the silver spoon and are incapable of understanding the blood, sweat, and toil my people have undergone: carrying tree trunks on their shoulders in unforgiving 107 degree sunlight, shoveling snow in negative 20 degree weather, and working 20 hour days in factory jobs just to put food on the table.

And what do you know of persecution? You don't know what it's like to be harassed by the cops because of the color of your skin; to be asked if you could speak English simply because of your last name; to be harassed on the street and called "wetback," "fence jumper," or "illegal;" and to be told, "Shut up, or I'll come up over there and slap the shit out of your little brown ass."

And what do you know of humiliation? You don't know what it's like to be 6 years old, digging through the trash at 5 in the morning just to earn money—and then hiding your face at school so no one would recognize you. You don't know what it's like to stand powerless behind your mother as she is scorned or what it's like to be degraded in front of your own children.

No, Trump. You know nothing of persecution and humiliation.

And make no mistake, *La Raza* is here, *La Raza* is proud, *La Raza* is strong. We have fought, worked, and studied in order to be free, and we will not tolerate attacks, insults, or needless persecution and humiliation, especially from chicken shit gringos who know nothing of the word.

You have unleashed the voice of Hidalgo, the bloody rage of the Aztecs, and the wrath of Villa.

Vete a la verga, pendejo. La Raza va hacer que te comas tus pinches palabras.

Kevin James
TRUMP & HIS BLOODSUCKERS

Like my mangy cat,
   who pulls the fur
from her hindquarters,
   her legs, hairless,
her neck in scabs,

our great nation now
   is infested with fleas,
which we must pick and pluck and bite
   until, at last, the poison comes.

Kevin James
T-RALLY

If you look out
   at your crowd,
your mouth to the mic,
   and they're beating someone,
fists to his face, feet
   to his ribs, know
you've turned bad bad bad,
   your voice
gone wrong, your soul
   split, spilt, spoiled, a mush.
Look up. God may not
   spite you with a golden
bolt, but I might.
   I just might.

Kyle Laws
IN ATLANTIC CITY

Across from Trump Taj Mahal
is what remains of historic Steel Pier,
and although what ended that eighty year run
was fire, not one of the Nor'easters that before
had threatened to do in the pier, so someone wrestled
the expanse of planks back to shore and fastened
it to pilings dug deep into shifting sands,
lit up the neon one more time,
and shepherded the diving horse into the elevator
that took it to the edge of what was once a ramp
that a blind girl rode galloping until the horse and rider
flung themselves into the air, and the crowd gasped,
and the horse steadied itself for the climb out
of the tank where they landed.

But Donald still called the line of carnival hawkers
offering stuffed toys and amusement rides "Steel Pier"
even though it was such a pale shadow of the original
you would have thought he'd be embarrassed
as you would have thought naming a hotel and casino
Taj Mahal when some of his neighbors lived
in tenements would have given him pause,
but he bankrupted the palace,
let it go down as the diving bell that once plunged
into the Atlantic for a murky view out portholes
at the end of Pennsylvania Avenue.

Jill Karno
THESE BURIED HEARTS

In Denver,
As a woman and her closest friends cry,

The world buries their hearts,
Leaving their songs unsung.

I pray
(To a god I do not know)

That these buried hearts
Turn into seeds,

And that the songs of their steady beats
Break the ground at every fault line.

Let the risen fall
And the fallen rise.

You
Will never be

Our
President.

Nadia Wolnisty
HOW THE LIGHT GETS IN

1.
I am in a burnt-up home in Lima, Ohio for on-the-site training. I'm an insurance adjuster, with boots and clipboard. The contractor tells me about the chemical sponges they are using to clean up smoke, the industrial blowers for the non-porous materials, and the huge drying fans for the damage done by the fire-department. So much has to be thrown away: cheap vinyl flooring (the cheapest you can get), baseboard, carpet, and drywall. I can see the studs, jack and king, cripple studs, and rafters. Thoroughly gutted, it's an umbrella that will protect no one.

2.
The contractor and I climb up on the roof. I feel like I'm climbing onto the back of a beached wale. I'm so high up with nothing to hold on to. The roof is gray and scabbed with strange, dry barnacles. It's a standard built-up roof with layers of asphalt that get cracked in snow and sun. Before the fire, this roof was badly damaged from years of neglect. The contractor tells me that apartment roofs are always neglected: out of sight, out of mind. "There is a crack in everything. That's how the light gets in."

3.
Leonard Cohen died yesterday, the day after election, when I had no choice but to look at burnt up homes.

4.
I don't know all the words to "Anthem," but I do know *The Pledge of Allegiance*. I learned it in school.

5.
No matter the cause of the fire, the cleaning process is largely the same: chemical sponges clean up smoke, industrial blowers for the non-porous materials, and huge drying fans for the damage done by the fire-department. On my hands and knees, back bent over, mask covering my face to keep me safe, I sing, under my breath, "That's how the light gets in."

I am in a burnt-up home in Lima, Ohio, trying to learn how to love America.

Ezhno Martín
HELL IS IN THE HEARTLAND

All the preachers and the politicians
        are telling the lies the public
                begged to have proven true
and meanwhile the matadors and the click-bait trappers
        are setting up their muletas and slide-shows
to hide the violence behind their veils

The plebeians are screaming down with the power
                and plugging into the grid
        The militarized police are keeping track
                and kicking in doors to suppress the blowback
        behind inconvenient facts

America the beautiful
        is being gargled from sea to squalid sea
through the bullshit every student is forced to swallow
        if they just hold their noses
it will taste good they're told

Cause it's the immigrant's stench
the greedy do-gooders and goddamn non-believers
it's the pacifist's demands and socialist's piracy
the sharecropper's arrogance and cripple's deficiencies

        Anything that suggests otherwise is a conspiracy

Conjecture and inference
        push the advertising algorithms
and anyway
                the status-quo has had enough
           of their copyright on power being stolen
              so the status is everything else is a lie
      across the dirt farming sister fucking corn-bread
                            heartland
                        because hell and handing over
the keys is on the horizon
        and they are ready to buy anything
                suggesting otherwise

Maryfrances Wagner
NOVEMBER AFTERMATH

I grabbed the scissors. The Exacto
could slice quicker, but scissors
could thin the oregano, unplug
a buried pebble, decapitate oak
starts with a single clip, half
the hornworm and the spider
babies busy eating it.
So much versatility excites me.
Have I aborted a Luna? An acorn?
Have I stopped a pebble's voice?
Snails stitch seams across the path
where we walk. Despite its tentacled
roving eye, it's still a slug. Fall is so
brown this year and eighty degrees.
My dog suspects nothing.
Many mysteries for her lie
beneath these dry leaves.

Alisha Escobedo
ANOTHER MODERN DECLARATION

My dearest love,
Let us bulldoze the borders between us
As we come together in flames.
One bashful, one brave,
But our genders are the same.
And when we come together, we are saved
From all of the rage that equates to the glory days.

My dearest love,
When I ravage your body,
I will do it as if you are America.
I will do it as if I have come to conquer you
From the cowards in charge.
I will wrap this flag around our naked bodies,
And we will ignite the stars,
Burning the hate out of every stitch
Until it is singed and charred.
I will do it as if I am overthrowing the government.
I will do it as if I am ridding you
Of the tyranny of frivolous leaders
Who think we have a choice,
Who think we can be changed,
Who think and think and think,
Who don't think our love is bathed.

And yet, my dearest love,
I shall love you like Millay's "Modern Declaration."
No matter what party is in power,
No matter what temporarily orange hue
Of policies wins the election,
I shall love you always.

Emma Fernout
LETTERS

dear apocalypse,
i'm sick of love letters. you're a sex scene; our eyes stray across your covers, dangerous. we like to flirt with you, study your every curve. you mudflap girl, you're looking hot on bumper stickers and magazines and the new york times bestseller list. red, white, and bruise looks good on you. turn us on. everyone wants to be the girl with the gun, the boy with the bomb; everyone wants be the hero of their story, twisting out the sky, wringing out the snow to trace memoirs into the ground. we've been ignoring the foreplay while waiting and waiting for you to come. surrounded by evidence of personal apocalypses, you got them on their knees praying "no" in a symphony of muffled pleas. please, turn this around; give it all a reason.

dear god,
by now, isn't it time to start over?

dear hate,
maybe i have always known you were here. i stood still, shower gone, water slinking down skin, feeling every single drop. we forget forecasts like fiction forgetting about an addiction, which is an oxymoron. but aren't we all? see, i've never remembered so many blood moons in one year, so many hunter moons, so many times we've almost come close and long. yet the moon keeps leaving. we just keep waning, just a decreasing reflection, infected.

dear tolerance,
i liked the idea of you until it started snowing, and the grey matter told us to tread softly, lest we disturb time with our footprints. they used to call eclipse like he calls wolf, except the wolves are domesticated now, and we know the sun will come back home. but sometimes we have to run and dance and make snow angels, regardless.

dear control,
i'm trying to find balance in being content with the answers i have while still searching for the ones i don't. i want a faith bigger than my cynicism. i want a belief bigger than the red fires on the side of every road. give me the honesty to see the kids who have stopped crying. open my eyes to look beyond myself. i'm on my knees. i want us alive.

dear hope,
i understand it. okay? i understand it must be difficult to let the clouds rain this hard and keep the sun shining too. i can't always find the rainbow, but every time i rub my eyes, i see colors. this must be what god meant by promises. the colors are still inside the rainbow, they aren't gone. and neither are we.

Jason Preu
RE: HATING YOU

From: America
To: America
CC: The Future

America hates you so much, America.

America will never be deep purple, only something like the grey-green tainted waters of the GNP.

America will never understand you, America, because America hates you, America.

America is a little sorry, a little sad, and a little surprised by this.

America hates your privilege, America, and your incompetence, too.

America hates your impossible dream, America; your loud, lonely, looming, threat of a dream.

America hates just getting along, America. America wants to get ahead, America, way ahead, so far ahead it can watch its own ass saunter down Main Street in some sweet, black, party pants, America.

America, America, America continues to be stuck in traffic while soft clouds whisper grey overtures overhead overall, America, America.

America wants to get all its tattoos of you removed by Lazlo Hollyfed-level lasers, America, or overwritten with something less complicated than you, America - maybe a black hole?

America hates thieves and liars, America, and its ministry of time travel has no hope of roping in Mick Jagger to paint a black solution to the problem of you. What America needs is more money/less money/no money/new money/old money!

America knows that checks and balances is code for cash in politics, America, and so America hates. Even the first peoples, the Americans before you, America, well, America hates you with a particular and peculiar and persistent malice. Yes, America hates all of you, America. Don't think you can hide behind Will Smith and Mr. T., America.

America hates your fly-over places and your cloistered-in concrete spaces and your OMG!, flip- flopping, hard-working, hip-hopping faces, America.

America can no longer tolerate your Facebook feed, America, so get your Kleenex ready when America unfriends you, America. One click and it's done and you won't even get an e-mail notification.

America's new faith is convenience, America, though at night, behind closed doors, America knows it hates ease and comfort along with everything else truly American, America.

America hates watching you on reality TV, America, and America thinks you are ignorant and undeserving and spoiled and rotten to the very core, America.

America wants you to be better, to know better, and to treat everyone better, America. Why won't you, America? America wants to know why you, America, don't. Can't you, America? Why can't you, America?

America hates your broken right and frightened left and

walled-off top and forgotten bottom, America.

America hates and mistrusts your applications, America, and the black-mirror storefronts beckoning for spare change, fighting for dulled, red eyeballs in Ritalin-suffused dead nights. America can no longer control America's bowels, America, and America needs America's help after sucking down beer and BBQ and Dorito after Dorito, America, America, Doritos and America, such a greasy pair; America hates it all with a delicious, orange, powdery rage.

America is the judge, America, and America is the jury, America, and you bet yer red, white, and blue BOMB POPS! that America is the executioner, too. America hates that, America.

America hates wearing so many hats and being so many things to so many people, hates it, and Just wants to be one thing, America: Great again, America! But America hates greatness and gratefulness, too, and don't even mention intellect or science or faith or love or moral truths that bite and leave marks to prove they were there.

America hates the new you and the old you and the now you, America—all at the same time! Tell America how such paradoxes are even possible, America. Speak to America, America, of your magical powers and your mythical, mystical essence. Spin America an American Fievel Tail of days past—the good ol' days with those good ol' boys never meaning no harm since the day America was born—fueled by blood and germs and steel, America. In trouble with the law, America. And how. How do. Hate how. America, hates how you do so famously, America, that America is going to amend your Constitution, America, going to amend it 40 more times over 40 long days until there is one final amendment with these words:

> No New Amendments for America Hates You. This document is complete and right and forever impervious to America, America. This Amendment,

as is, now stands quiet in the uncut swamp grass that probes from the Disney dust corners of the Oval Office, stewing and simmering like green meat under red heat.

America hates—won't stand for—your protest poems, America, not since 1997. And surely without bookstores America makes known to America that yer furry, ragged howls ain't welcome 'round these parts no more, no how.

America hates seeing its best minds destroyed by sadness, America, raving bored through your meaningless streets, America, bath salts and Big Gulps, tattooed and tongue-tied. America begs you for answers, America, but all you have these days are questions and shiny distractions, which America hates about you, America, hates so hard.

America hates your blackness, America, and your yellowness and brownness and redness, too. And let's be honest, America, America hates your blank, quiet whiteness, hates it. Unless your whiteness is a chewy center wrapped around by lush, green silks, America hates you, America. You read that at the start, America, but it bears repeating way down here, too.

America hates, yes, truly abhors, your fired, your poor, all your huddled masses, masses of any type, truly, truly, America, America. America smirks and refuses to open its golden door to anymore tempest-tost wretched masses, America. You might be a star tonight, America, so let that camera roll. You're the red, white and blue, America. Oh the funnyfunnyfunny things you do, America.

America, America, America ...

What are you?

PART THREE
THE DISENFRANCHISED

.chisaraokwu. (naijabella)
MY BLOOD FLOWS RED

There is a lump in my throat
that carries the weight of tears not yet shed,
of words that refuse to be uttered,
of fears that make this body tremble.

Oh! — that I would be a surgeon,
skilled with blade and steady hand,
and excise this growing tyranny within me!

To see my blood flow red and know
that I yet live (and that I am human),
and to place this thing
into your callous hands so you might see
that my blood flows red (and that I yet live)
and that I, too, am human!

MG Salazar
MY ANCESTORS' BLOOD

i have been to many countries
i have been on four continents

rambling the world
is my activity of choice

i am asked how i am
i am asked for directions
i am asked what restaurant is good
i am asked how to work this coffee machine
i am asked where i got my coat

i don't always understand these questions
(the languages in which they're delivered)
but I understand a look of kinship

and the only place i've been told to "go home"
is on the land that holds my ancestors' blood

Miguel M. Morales
THIS POEM ISN'T

This poem isn't going to
save the world, yours or mine.

This poem isn't going to
stop the pussy-grabbing or the tweets.

This poem isn't going to
end the Heil Trumps and the Lock Her Ups.

This poem isn't going to
change the electoral college or the gerrymandering.

This poem isn't going to
make the streets safe from bashings and harassment.

This poem isn't going to
shred the confederate flag or rebuild Black churches.

This poem isn't going to
eradicate the symbols of lynchings and white supremacy.

This poem isn't going to
dismantle the wall and English only laws.

This poem isn't going to
prevent mass deportations and the incarceration of children.

This poem isn't going to
forbid Muslim registries and internment camps.

This poem isn't going to
safeguard your family, teach your children, ensure your
freedom, protect your water, extinguish hate, or save your life.

You are.

Jessica Ayala
SEEDS

A young seventh generation warrior shouts, *"Si se puede!"*

His arm rises to the sky;
fist meets the Black Panther moon.

We dance to Mother Earth tonight.

Sacred drum names the spirits of
Sandra,
Michael,
Trayvon,
Oscar,
Fred, and Emmet.

Sacred fires sing medicine songs to a Black mother's cry.

Mother Earth cries too.

You are my daughter's Mexica skin color,
organic Oceti Sakowin clay.

They caged you in dog kennels,
my sister,
as you watched them eat strange fruit,
much like the cages of Eloy.

Long before the rock of North Dakota
stood in below-freezing temperatures,
Sitting Bull felt the waters
of the same hoses once used in the South.

Mní Wíconí,
we are the same clay red
bearing the fruit of our ancestors.

We are seeds,
watered to be planted
and replanted again,
bearing fruit to decolonize the word
strange.

Decolonize the word
Bland,
Brown,
Martin,
Grant,
Hampton,
Till.

We shall not be moved.

We lift every voice
so that
We the People
can still hear
the
bells
of
freedom.

Iriquois Pliskin
A LETTER TO PRESIDENT OBAMA

Dear President Obama,

For thirteen years, I lived in fear as if I were a hermit. I lived in society but was not part of it. During that time, I was left behind while my friends, classmates, and siblings found jobs, were married, pursued careers, and started families. I felt like a prisoner in my own home. All of that changed when you created DACA. Finally, I was able to get my driver's license, a job, and become a contributing member of society. Finally, I was able to live like a normal person and feel like a human being. Thank you for creating the DACA program. I am so grateful to you.

When I first learned that I was eligible for DACA (and what it could do for me), I couldn't believe it. But I also thought it might be a trick. Wounds from the rejection of the Dream Act were still fresh in my mind. As I sat in my immigration attorney's office not knowing what to say, cracks in my stoic expression started to form and all of my bottled up emotions burst out like a dam with too much pressure. I lost all control of my emotions and began to cry.

She asked, "Why are you crying?"

"I don't want to be filled with false hope," I replied.

Then, she explained that the DACA was an executive order by the president and that no one could take it away.

The day I received news that my application had been approved —and that my work permit was already on its way—was one of the happiest moments of my life. It meant that, finally, I could get the thing that I wanted most: a driver's license. The next morning I drove to DMV with everything I needed:

Employment Authorization Document, Social Security Card, and confirmation from the state of Kansas.

It was a rainy day, so I thought not many people would want to take a driving test that day, but by the time I arrived, there was already a long line of people. Two hours later, my number was called. I was nervous but hopeful as I stated my intentions: "Yes. I want to take both the written and driving tests." The clerk typed on the computer, took my picture, and handed me the bill. "That'll be $24, please!" But I only had only $16 in my wallet. I had forgotten about the picture fee.

I decided that I was not going to wait one more day for my driver's license. I was so close to my goal, yet it seemed so far away. As I left the DMV to get more money, my heart was on the verge of popping out of my chest. I hoped that I could make it home and back without being pulled over, which I did. I passed both the written and driving tests on the first try. And as soon as I returned home, I started looking for a job.

For the past four years I've been working and taking acting classes. I haven't made it to Hollywood yet but maybe someday. I just wanted to say thank you. All of this has been made possible by your actions. We have never met, but you've made a huge difference in my life, more than you can imagine.

Even though now that the future looks grim, I do not regret applying for the DACA. Thank you, Mr. President.

Sincerely,

Iriquois Pliskin

Keith D. Wilson
RISING UP

our great nation
was built with hard work
and remarkable ingenuity

on a lasting foundation
of brutal conquest
and broken treaties

on the bent, beaten backs
of black slaves
working the fields

on generations
of dirt-poor coal miners'
broken spirits and ruint lungs

in the wombs
of women raising children
for their rapists

on the profits
of selling bombs and guns
for perpetual war

with cheap fuel
ripped from the ground
and spewed into the ecosystem

five hundred years
of toxic sludge
pollutes our psyches

long buried and denied
it is now rising up
in ugly boils and pustules

can we find within
the ability to embrace
to forgive and heal this darkness

or will the rising dark
overwhelm and envelop
leading inexorably to violent

up rising

Iris Appelquist
DON'T BE A FUCKING RACIST

Now, more than ever, it is important to actively, openly, and consistently reject bigoted and sexist attitudes in the public sphere. Secret symbols are fine—important and necessary—but so are loud, blatant statements. If you enjoy privilege in America, then it is your responsibility to use it and begin moving past an insane history of genocidal, racist patriarchy.

Alisha Escobedo
THE POWER OF PUSSY

The power of pussy will prevail over the power of a coward with cash. Calloused and brash, are we to submit to a man that calls his own flesh and blood a raw piece of ass? Rotten and crass, muddling the world until we're all as bitter as a soul that's been lost in a flask. This is our system: submit to the vision of men with their dicks in their hands who tell you that you can't when you can, who make laws about bodies they don't understand, who think they don't have to ask to put their hands in the sand that covers the pearls of women and girls who are trying to swim while being drowned within and on land. Submit to the man. A man. Any man. Give him the warmth of your loaded body but don't take away the cold that cocks and then jams, cocks and then jams, as he fingers the trigger and then frolics unmanned into the sunset. If only we could unman the undeserving men—castrate them against their wills. Mr. Money-havin'-pussy-grabbin', if you don't have to ask, then we won't either. We will incite the fever that burns holes into our lace panties as we chase dandelions in fields made of aged wisdom that is no longer wise at all. And, really, why should we be surprised at all? Let us rise above the silent love and let us speak loudly; let us proudly feel our pulses as they beat against our wrists and necks, reminding us that we are still alive to stand and speak and feel and be more than they want us to be. Yes, the power of pussy prevails over the power of a coward with cash, and there is no price that can buy this pussy, Mr. President-elect.

Nichole Force
BOXING HILLARY

Following the election, there was much made in the media about the fact that a majority of white women (53%) cast their votes for Trump. Why would so many women vote for such an openly sexist man who has an unapologetic history of being verbally and physically abusive to their gender? A good metaphor for this phenomenon is the movie, *Boxing Helena*, in which the protagonist amputates the arms and legs of a woman he's obsessed with so he can control and keep her to himself. She is strong, self-assured and defiant, and she fights back, criticizes, and attacks him throughout most of the movie. But near the end, she comes to accept her fate, grows more docile, and even begins to feel love for him thanks to the way he "takes care of" her.

Throughout history, women have been maimed physically to appease and appeal to men, from foot-binding to female genital mutilation to extensive cosmetic surgery. But they've also been maimed psychologically, intellectually and emotionally through the verbal abuse and degradation they experience on an almost daily basis from our culture, media, and men like Trump. This kind of maiming is not as visible but is just as damaging and limiting as the physical kind. Like Helena, no matter how strong women may have been at one point, eventually they get ground down into a space where the only viable option seems to be accepting what's been done to them and making the best of it because they feel helpless to change it.

This very thing is what makes Hillary's defeat so tragic. She was clearly the most qualified candidate (endorsed by all five living ex-presidents and every major publication in the country and absolutely destroyed Trump in all three debates), but yet she still could not pull herself up out of that space in order to beat an openly offensive man with no political experience whatsoever and unbridled disdain for women. If Hillary, one of the most brilliant and strong women our country has ever known, could not do it, then what message does that send to other women trying to overcome (and realize) their full potential in this deeply sexist world?

Too many women refuse to escape the box that's been fashioned for them by the men who wish to contain their power and exploit their bodies. A vote for a man is a vote for someone to take care of their hobbled, broken bodies and minds — bodies and minds they have been brainwashed to believe were broken from the start. There are far too many Helenas in this world, and the real tragedy is that they don't even realize it. And they vote.

Andrea Caspari
A STUDENT DREW A SWASTIKA INTO MY COPY OF <u>NIGHT</u>

Hoping the Holocaust remains history and doesn't slip into current events, I will evoke pleasure from this pain, put the *ART* in catharsis, soothe these wounds with the words of Elie Wiesel:

> Never shall I forget that night, the first night in the camp, which has turned my life into one long night, seven times cursed and seven times sealed. Never shall I forget the little faces of the children, whose bodies I saw turned into wreaths of smoke beneath a silent blue sky.

I will never be desensitized.
The photos. The footage. The reality.

How can I read this horror to children?
Oh, G-d ... How can I NOT?

What if they turn this into a joke?
What if they never learn the story behind the smoke?
What if I find a swastika on page 47?

Skeletal bodies.
Grandmothers hugging mothers hugging babies.
Cattle car. Crying out in the night.

"How could they do this to us?" To us.

Cattle car coming for us.
My grandmother hugging mother hugging baby.

Aunt Frida's bracelet slides down, revealing faded numbers from a ghastly lottery.

Grandma Rachel escaped in '33 to her Moon Over
Uhlandstrasse, evading the Third Reich on the Third Night.

Grandpa Sam escaped, hiding in Italy for two years; loaves of
bread tossed mercifully into a wine vat, a prisoner of a war.
No one understands The Way Out.

His parents didn't make it. Somehow, I did.
I am here to tell their story. Their story is my story.
And now, that story is more important than ever.

The fascism. The rhetoric.
The refugees. The registering.
Making the country great.
And that's just the Republican debate.

A man with funny hair comes 'round every 50 years and takes
advantage of your tears.

Don't follow the sheep, or your people will end up like mine:
in that heap.

I will not hide behind that "silent blue sky."
I will speak my mind and give you some truth to get behind.

It happened to us. It can happen again. Don't fool yourself,
my friend.

Speak. Act. Vote. If you don't register ... they'll register you.

My name is Andrea Caspari ... and I am a Jew.

Kathryne Husk
AKTION T4

i am
the 275,000 disabled
murdered
in the holocaust

i am
lebensunwertes leben
"life unworthy of life"

i see you
shake your head
in vehement
disagreement

except ...

i don't believe you
because you killed me

they used
your objectifying pity
and your perverted
sense of compassion
against me

they said it was god's will
and you nodded your head
compliant
appealing to your belief
that i am less

you tell me
you disagree

except ...

the inspirational articles
(um, i mean
eugenics propaganda)
you keep spreading
on facebook
(um, i mean
in nazi films)
and street corners
and shop windows
tell me otherwise

you promised me
i would be safe
because this is america
(um, i mean
germany)
and there are
checks and balances

except ...

it didn't matter

they compassionately
piled me
in a compassionate
mass grave

after all
it's the compassionate
nationalist thing to do

(and in the end
saves the state money
to do more
of god's work)

2016
(um, i mean
1941)
has been a truly horrible year
for the disabled

Nazi Propaganda slide featuring a disabled infant. The caption reads: "... because God cannot want the sick and ailing to reproduce."

James Inman
REPUBLICANS V. DEMOCRATS

September 11, 2001
Republicans: "All Muslims are terrorists!"
Democrats: "All Muslims are terrorists!"

Iraq War 2003
Republicans: "All Muslims are terrorists!"
Democrats: "Not all Muslims are terrorists!"

Iraq War 2005
Republicans: "All Muslims are terrorists!"
Democrats: "Where are those weapons of mass destruction?"

Election 2008
Republicans: "Obama is a Muslim!"
Democrats: "Would you please shut the fuck up?"

Election 2012
Republicans: "Obama is a Muslim. All Muslims are terrorists!"
Democrats: "Please fucking let it go!"

Election 2016
Republicans: "Gays, blacks, Mexicans! All Muslims are terrorists!"
Democrats: "Oh shit! We are fucked!"

Paul Oldham
MUCH WORSE

I grew up around bullies, and at a few points in my life, I probably have been a bully too. When I was in high school in Arkansas, I was terrified of who I might be and frightened that I was going to be damned to hell. I screamed at God to answer my prayers. School classmates tortured and harassed me just for being "different," and for many years, I was suicidal. After I started coming out, it only got worse.

My youth pastor was unprepared to counsel a gay kid. He asked about my relationship with my father and eventually set up a meeting with my parents with the intention of outing me. Otherwise, I wouldn't have come out to my parents at 18. At first, my parents tried to be supportive. I invited them to attend a PFLAG meeting, but they declined. Our relationship would take several dark turns before it improved.

But many of my friends went through things MUCH WORSE than I did. I am very lucky that I wasn't sent to conversion therapy. And if I had come out earlier, then bad science—influenced by bad religion—could have left me with more scars than I already have.

After not feeling particularly accepted in my childhood, I, as an adult, ran into the arms of the first person who gave me the acceptance I craved: an abusive and manipulative addict with demons of his own. And together, I'm sure, our combined demons made hell in both of our lives.

Now, after waging my own fight for basic rights, dignity, respect, and value, I finally fit into this world. And let me tell you this: every second of every day we will watch this bully in the White House. We will fight for the right of women to be autonomous over their bodies and not allow the government to dictate what they can and can't do with them. We will fund the shit out of NASA, by donation if need be. We will vote the hell out of the midterm elections and gain back our seats. We will dismantle the Democratic establishment and from its ashes create a new Phoenix on the wings of Bernie Sanders and Elizabeth Warren. And we will congratulate Hillary Clinton for a job well done in winning the popular vote.

And we will grab America's "deplorables" by the motherfucking pussy.

We won't even wait.

Benjamin Rosenthal
THIS IS ...

This is not about making America great again; this is about tipping the scales in favor of those who, in their own worlds, are so insecure and pathetic that they can't accept that others might be lifted too.

This is about fragile, straight white male egos who are angry that they don't make more money than their much smarter or capable black and brown neighbors; this is about white supremacists ratifying open hunting season on young black and brown men and women, who they still believe should be slaves picking cotton.

This is about driving *faggots* back into the closet (where they think we apparently belong), denying us housing, and the right to live freely and safely; this is about beating the shit out of LGBTQIA people in an attempt to enforce their outdated, so-called Christian values.

This is about reducing women to their genitalia, rejecting the superiority of their intelligence, capability, and strength, and denying them equal pay for equal work, which threatens the supremacy of the straight white male ego; this is about putting Susan B. Anthony in her damn place.

This is about not trusting a woman who is smart and capable; this is about trusting a monster who has time and time again, bankruptcy after bankruptcy, demonstrated that he can't be trusted.

This is about an America without greatness; this is a day about rage.

Ezhno Martín
IN JUNK YARD DOGS WE TRUST

Through all the screaming and gnashing of the teeth on the eve of another totalitarian regime taking power, I try to remember how it felt to believe that it was all going to get better four years ago, a decade ago.

I remember last year being called a *faggot*, being blind sided with a fist, and being pushed in the snow.

I remember last month my co-worker saying "lazy nigger" and looking at me like she thought I'd been thinking it too.

I remember how many times I've started a sentence with "I'd like to" and how few times that sentence has ended with "love her since birth."

I remember how few times I've spoken up when all the talk of sluts makes me just a little sick to my stomach.

I remember what violence tastes like from both sides.

I remember yesterday standing in line to buy pepper spray, about to head to the rich part of town to burn some old right-winger's eyes right out of his fucking skull in retribution for voting for war and hate, when irony pushed the bile up my throat and me into a sickened introspection.

I remember how almost every dog I've ever met has been scared and confused and desperate to be loved but leads with their teeth because that's what they've been taught to do.

Fear leads to hate. Always has. Always will. That's why we have a government. Because beneath it all, much more than we can't trust each other, we know we can't trust ourselves.

CC Grooms
THE EMPEROR'S NEW CLOTHES

I dig out from under the
Don't-Give-A-Fuck pile a few things shed
(when I slipped into
something-a-little-more-comfortable,
a little more Gender Queer),
during the hard-earned luxury of Obama's regime.

With quick, darting swipes,
dusting off years of intolerance, I redress in
the stains of moldering glances, sticky, hurtful words,
soul-deep burns, and muck too stuck to quit.
I pray that this uniform will
avoid catching the
(unwanted, unsolicited, non-consensual)
eye of an Alt-Right informant,
attention I cannot afford.

Looking in the mirror, my heart begins the
tamponade of the New World Order call,
set to the sounds of shattering morals.

Max Martin
SAINT JUDE THADDEUS

You made me
This way from the dirt floors of your childhood home
Shards of your mother who left you with an empty table

You taught me
To be the biggest tomato
And how to gut fish so that I'd be a hunter too

You told me
Stories of picking strawberries for five cents a quart
And how the oldest of a litter has to take care of the baby

You helped me
Fall in love with love and gave me enough courage to fill a room
Even enough to tell you when I'd had enough of you

You're the kind of guy
Who chose war before it chose you
The same guy who chose war for me

Now, I'm staring down the barrel of a loaded gun
Your finger is on the trigger and it seems you can't remember
That I was once the daughter you endlessly prayed for

My cause is lost to you
For out in the corn fields
Faggots keep quiet

Special thanks to Jenny Wise and her friends on the Pine Ridge Reservation for providing the wonderful photos that appear on the front cover and interior of this anthology.

www.ingramcontent.com/pod-product-compliance
Lightning Source LLC
Chambersburg PA
CBHW021446080526
44588CB00009B/708